Kite decoratic  *its*

Designing and decorating kites is both fun and creative. It offers infinite scope for individual expression and originality. Within the basic range of the sixteen different principles of kite design illustrated in section two, there are any number of variations possible. In fact, most kite designs derive from one of these basic principles. It is therefore possible to develop original kites, designing your own structural system by using an appropriate basic form and applying the rules of symmetry and balance. And there are as many ways of decorating them as there are few limiting rules.

Basic rules of decoration

1. Structure
An important design consideration is the relationship between the structural pattern and the decoration of the kite. The decoration, figurative or abstract, should always relate strongly to the kite's basic form. Some Japanese kites take this ideal to superb extremes with the decoration dictating the form.

2. Design
There is one particular graphic consideration to keep in mind. You should remember that the design on the kite will be seen at a distance and so should be simple and bold in general layout, but could have delicate detailing within the bold outlines.

3. Colour
The distance also affects the way in which colours are perceived – they tend to lose their strength, and this together with the silhouetting effect of the kite against the light sky makes the colours seem darker and weaker. To compensate you should use strong, clear colours, containing as little grey as possible.

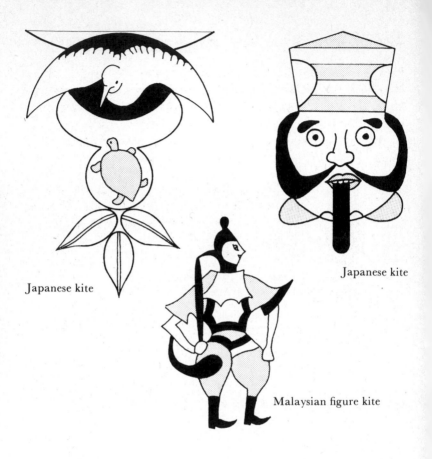

Japanese kite

Japanese kite

Malaysian figure kite

Movement can be employed as a strong visual element – fluttering edges, waving fronds, revolving discs, and even more simply, on a 3-dimensional kite like a box, the movement of one plane in front of another. This effect may be heightened by the use of vivid complementary colours against each other, (blue and orange; red and green; etc.), or even using a simplified moiré pattern on transparent PVC.

Kite attachments

Here is a list of kite attachments which can be fun but must also obey the rules of symmetry and balance – for example you must attach an equal number of tassels to each side of the kite otherwise it will fly lopsidedly.

Tails – bunched, folded, tasselled.

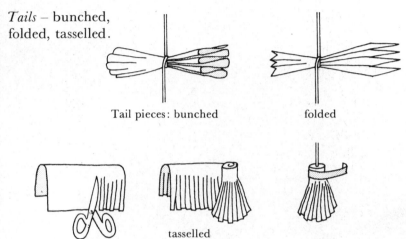

Tail pieces: bunched   folded

tasselled

Festoonings – almost anything that is light and decorative – paper streamers, tinsel, feathers, dried grasses/leaves.

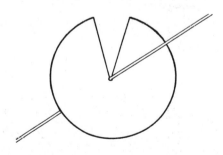

Paper messenger

Lights – weight is the problem here – don't overload the kite with battery and bulb circuits, and remember balance. But lights can produce an exciting effect at night.

Fireworks – sparklers are best, with a fuse to enable the kite to rise high before they ignite, but consider well the fire-risk both to your kite and others' property.

Parachute – this is blown up the kite line and when the line is jerked the messenger releases the parachute and it floats gently down.

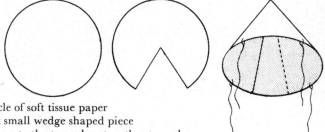

Parachute
(a) Cut circle of soft tissue paper
(b) Cut out small wedge shaped piece
(c) Lightly paste the two edges together to make cone shape. Attach four 60 cm long threads at equal intervals round the rim

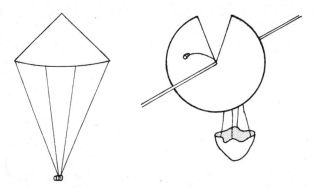

(d) Hold parachute tip and knot threads together at bottom. Attach small weight
(e) Fix parachute and messenger to kite line as shown

Music attachments

Buzzers – take a strip of paper and glue one edge round a string or spar. Cut a fringe in the strip so that it will vibrate in the wind, creating a buzzing noise.

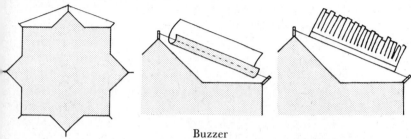

Buzzer

Hummers – add a bowed spar to the back of the kite. The bow should be tied with piano-wire or a guitar string. It is possible to fit several hummers to one kite so that a harmony is produced.

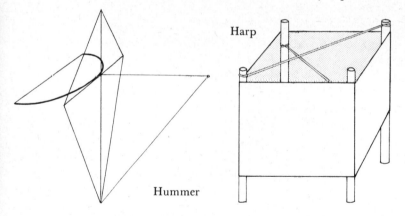

Harp

Hummer

Harps – on a box-kite, stretch metal strings of different thicknesses across one or both ends without allowing them to touch each other. The strings will vibrate in the wind producing a pleasant sound.

Pipes – tie 'penny-whistles' or pan-pipes to one of the spars, making sure that the mouthpieces are facing into the wind.

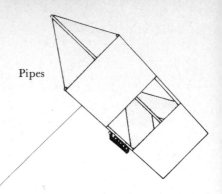

Pipes

Photography from kites

It is possible, by means of a camera suspended from the frame, to use a kite for the purpose of aerial photography. This was successfully done at the turn of the century by meteorologists and army technicians wishing to observe the enemy without endangering lives. Photography from aeroplanes has largely made the technique outmoded, but there are still instances where a photograph taken from a kite can be a better (and less expensive) method than photographs taken from an aeroplane – photographing a house in a built-up area for instance. For the keen photographer it can be an interesting, and sometimes surprising experience.

When first experimenting with kite photography, it would be wise to use a cheap camera until you have mastered the skills involved. Make sure that the camera is securely attached to the frame and is pointing in the right direction for the photographs you wish to take. When positioning the camera on the frame remember that the kite dips forward in flight. Early experimenters used various ingenious devices for releasing the shutters of their cameras, including slow-burning fuses and explosions. You might like to experiment with some of these methods, or even devise your own. A simple device is to arrange a rubber-band so that it will jerk the shutter across or release it, depending on the type of camera you are using. Then relieve the shutter from the pull of the rubber band by a string to which a fuse is attached. Alternatively, attach a time-release mechanism to the camera, or, if you are lucky enough to have one, use a motor-driven camera that will automatically take photographs at pre-set time intervals.

Glossary diagrams

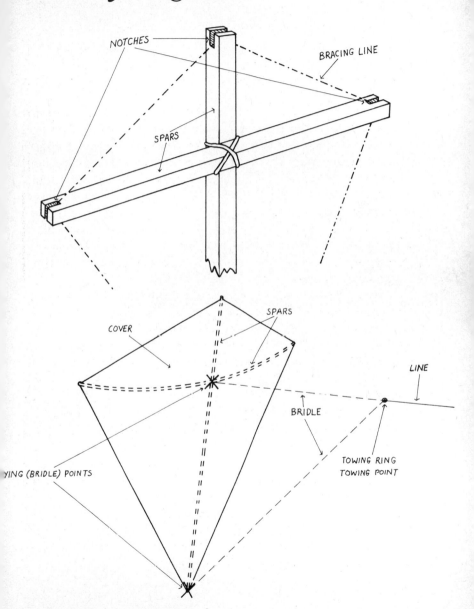

NOTCHES

BRACING LINE

SPARS

COVER

SPARS

LINE

BRIDLE

YING (BRIDLE) POINTS

TOWING RING
TOWING POINT

Section 2

Materials and structure

Sixteen kites to make

Material	Lightness	Wind resistance	Ease of use	Hardwearing
Silk	+	✓	×	✓
Silk substitute	✓	○	×	✓
Lightweight nylon	✓	○	×	✓
Closely woven cotton	○	○	○	✓
PVC sheet	✓	+	+	✓
Spinnaker sail	+	✓	○	+
Fibrous tissue	✓	○	✓	○
Tissue paper	✓	○	✓	×
Rice paper	✓	○	✓	×
Brown wrapping paper	○	○	✓	○
Polystyrene tiles	+	+	✓	×
Crepe paper	○	○	✓	○

Key
Very good +
Good ✓
Moderate ○
Poor ×

Materials

Cover materials

The selection of materials for making a kite will depend not only on their suitability but also on availability and cost. Silk, for instance, is a practical material to use for covers being light and strong, but is expensive. Whereas brown wrapping paper, not only a cheap and a commonly available material, is also strong and light enough to make a good cover.

Covers can, and have been made of such widely differing materials as polystyrene, spinnaker sail, old newspaper, leaves and even old umbrella covers. It might be helpful to list some of the more readily available and suitable materials under the criteria they should fulfil: see table on page 49.

Spars

Light square-section hardwood, or softwood, is a particularly good material for kite spars provided it is free from knots and defects. It has the advantage of being easily obtainable – both from model shops and timber merchants.

Most kites in this book use square-section spars but bamboo can easily be substituted if more easily obtained. If bamboo is used it is important that corresponding struts on the kite are of exactly the same thickness and strength so that the kite is balanced. The pieces may need some work on them shaving off irregularities with a sharp knife before they are ready to use. Not only is bamboo a strong, flexible wood, but the fact that it is hollow makes it lighter than solid timber. Another useful quality of bamboo is that it can be bent without breaking, and the bend may be fixed without tying by waving the bent bamboo strip over a small flame and then allowing it to cool.

Most Chinese and Japanese kites use bent bamboo strips and

certainly this is the material you should use for making complicated small kites such as insect kites. In the West the best way of obtaining this form of bamboo is to buy a bamboo slatted dinner mat or window blind as this saves all the hard work needed to prepare the material.

Thin-walled aluminium and duranium alloy tubes have a particularly good strength/weight ratio. They do, however, have their drawbacks, their relatively high cost not least among

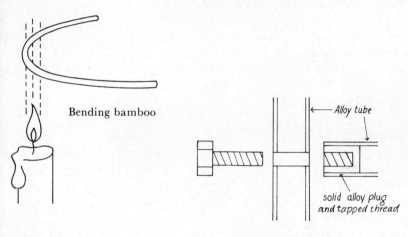

Bending bamboo

Alloy tube

solid alloy plug and tapped thread

Cross-section of screw-fix method of joining alloy tubes

them. They also need some ingenuity to join together. Welding, for instance, is an obvious choice; but not many people have access to the equipment needed. A screw-fix is probably one of the most effective ways of joining, and this has the added advantage of being demountable. It should be said that a kite made with this kind of care and with such high performance materials as alloy tube and spinnaker sail will result in a superb soaring machine.

51

Adhesives

Paper and Tissue:
Tissue paste
Home-made flour paste
Petroleum based glue
Double-sided adhesive tape

Cloth (if not sewn):
Light rubber based glues
Vinyl-based glues

PVC Sheet:
Adhesive tape
Welder. Where many PVC kites are to be made, at a school for example, it might be economical to buy a small welding machine.

Line

Lightweight nylon line is the cheapest and most practical type of line available and can be used for all purposes. It can be obtained in many weights and thicknesses. For small kites choose a line with a breaking strain of 11 or 23 kg. For large kites a line with a breaking strain of 43 to 91 kg is best. Alternatively fishing line is a good material to use and has the advantage of being readily available. Ordinary household string can be used but it is sometimes rather heavy for a small kite. Never use a wire because this can conduct electricity from the atmosphere.

Tools

Very few tools are required for successful kite making. The following list contains all that is needed for making the kites illustrated in this book:

Fine saw – dovetail or hacksaw
Scissors
Long ruler
Large-eyed needle
Craft knife
Dress-making pins

Flying accessories

It is useful to have the following items with you when flying your kite, either to aid your flying or to make small repairs:

Reel or winding bobbin
Gloves – in strong winds the line can become very difficult to hold, and can give severe and painful hand burns. So wear strong gloves. It is possible to buy gardening gloves quite cheaply and these are good for kite flying.
Scissors or a knife
Needle and cotton (for repairing pockets)
Adhesive tape

Reels

It is possible to make a kite fly to moderate heights with no other equipment than a stick on which to wind the string or line. However, to fly a kite to a great height and to bring it successfully back to earth is much easier if you have a reel. Winding in without a reel becomes a chore, taking a long time, and is not much fun. A reel overcomes this difficulty and is so easy to make that any keen kite-flier should make one. The only tool you'll need apart from those already mentioned is a drill.

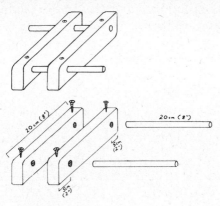

Winding bobbin
(The handles are secured
by screws)

Winding bobbin

A winding bobbin is easier to make than a reel and while not being so good for a long line is considerably better than a stick.

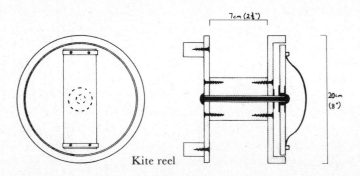

Kite reel

Kite construction

The instructions on how to make the kites in this section follow a step by step sequence. First we show a drawing of the finished kite to show you how it should look, with dimensions in centimetres. We also give a cutting list of the materials to be used, like the list of ingredients in a recipe for a cake.

In the set of diagrams, the kite skeleton or structure is shown first; then the lengths of spars required; this is followed by the joints or tying of the spars. The flat shape of the cover with dimensions is shown next; then how to seam or edge it; then its construction and pockets etc. We then show how the frame and the cover fit together and are secured, and finally the way in which the bridle is tied.

The sixteen kites we have chosen represent a cross-section of all the basically different types of kite available and they are arranged in order of complexity of construction. The simple Malay is therefore first and the complex multicell tetrahedral kite last.

Some of the main elements of construction common to all models are listed below. These should be studied carefully before you attempt to make any of the kites.

Notches

If a kite frame requires a bracing line, the ends of the spars will need to be notched. To make a notch saw a narrow slot $\frac{1}{2}$ cm deep at the end of the spar. Alternatively for bamboo cut a V-shaped notch also $\frac{1}{2}$ cm deep.

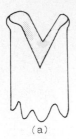 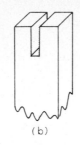 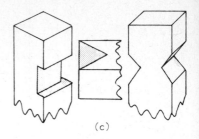

(a)   (b)   (c)

(a) V-shaped notch for bamboo
(b) Slot notch for square-section hardwood/softwood
(c) Other types of notches required for some kites

Cross-bracing

To join two cross-spars, place the spars together to the angle required and hold them in place. Wind string tightly round the crossing point and hold it, there is no need to tie a knot. When enough string to hold the spars securely has been used (ten or twelve turns should be enough) cover the joint with quick-drying glue for a really secure joint.

If there are three spars crossing over at one point, join two as above and then add the third. Where four spars cross, make two sets of two and then join these together in the same way.

Cross bracing

56

Knots

The following knots and tying methods are used:

   (a) *Reef knot:* a general   (b) *Bowline:* useful and reliable
         purpose knot   for tying kite lines to bridle

Bowing

Some kites require a bowed surface to give them stability. To bow a spar cut a notch 1 cm from each end of the spar before attaching the cover. After the cover has been attached to the frame cut a piece of string a little longer than the spar that is to be bowed. Lie the kite face down and tie the string to one end using the notch to stop the string slipping along the spar. Bend the spar gently to the required curve and tie the string to the notch at the other end of the spar.

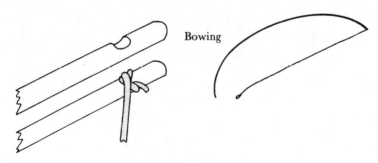

Bowing

Covers

The best and simplest method of cutting out a kite's cover is to place the finished kite frame on to the cover material, making sure that the material is laid flat, without folds or creases. Then, using the frame as a template, mark round its edge with chalk or a felt pen. It is important to leave an extra 2 cm hem all round for fixing the cover to the frame. If a cloth cover is being used make sure that the direction of the weave is from top to bottom and side to side, and in no other direction.

When using glue, read the instructions on the container to find out the approximate drying time. Don't use too much glue, it doesn't make the kite any more efficient. The best glues for attaching a cover to the frame are 'impact' adhesives, where after the glue has been spread on the surfaces, the two parts are set aside to dry slightly, and are then pressed firmly together, binding immediately.

If the cover is to be sewn, it is best to use a sewing machine for a neater and stronger join.

In some cases, particularly large kites designed to fly in heavy winds, it is better to nail the cloth cover to the frame with small tacks. Do this by turning the hem once round a spar and then place tacks at regular intervals down the whole length of the spar.

Cutting and
attaching cover

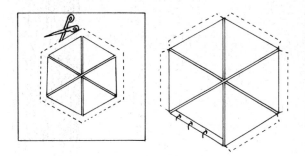

Bridles

The short strings from the kite to the main flying line are called the bridle. The function of the bridle is to hold the kite at the correct angle to the wind while it is flying.

Some kites, a box kite for example, will fly quite well with-

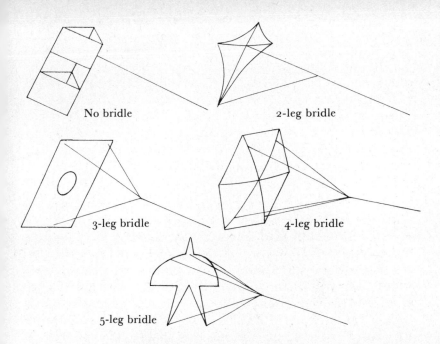

No bridle

2-leg bridle

3-leg bridle

4-leg bridle

5-leg bridle

out a bridle, the tying point being carefully chosen so that the wind and gravitational forces maintain a satisfactory flying angle. Most kites, however, require a two-, three- or four-leg bridle.

To make the bridle, strengthen the cover at the points shown on the individual kite instructions. This may be done with paper reinforcing circles on paper kites, adhesive tape on PVC covers, and extra squares of material on cloth covers. Pierce the strengthened cover and tie the bridle string round the spar behind. The instructions for each individual kite will tell you how long that string should be.

For a two-leg bridle, attach one end of the string to one of the tying points and loop (see diagram) the string through a small metal towing ring (a curtain ring or small washer is ideal) before tying the other end down. For a three-leg bridle, use two lengths of string, one of which is tied to the ring itself. If a four-leg bridle is required, use two crossing strings, looping them both through the towing ring.

The position of the towing ring can be adjusted by sliding it

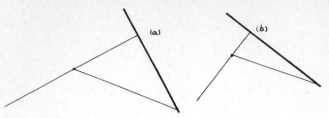

Bridle for normal wind conditions
The bridle is tied higher for strong winds

along the strings. The ring will remain in position when the line and bridle are made taut.

The kite should lean forward into the wind. If the towing point is too low, the kite will fly vertically and will not rise; if it is too high, the kite will fly at too low an angle and will flutter and behave in a generally erratic manner. In strong winds the kite generally needs to fly at a lower angle of attack, 'flatter' to the ground. So the towing-ring should be adjusted for weather conditions before each flight. The position of towing-rings in all construction diagrams is set for moderate wind conditions.

Tails

When making tails, it is important to remember that it is length and not weight that helps balance a kite. Generally a tail should be five times the height of the kite frame to give it proper stability, although this length may need varying a little for different conditions.

Attaching bridle to tying
point

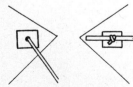

Looping the string through
the towing ring

Malay kite

Although a traditional Eastern kite, it was developed in the West by Eddie in the late nineteenth century and was used extensively in meteorological research of the upper atmosphere, determining temperatures and pressure. It flies very well in moderate and high winds.

Materials required

Spars – square section hardwood or softwood
One spar 90 cm × 0.6 cm
One spar 84 cm × 0.6 cm

Cover 90 cm × 90 cm
Lightweight cloth or tissue paper or crepe paper

Line
Glue
Towing ring

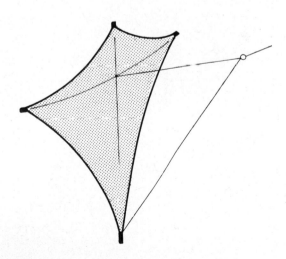

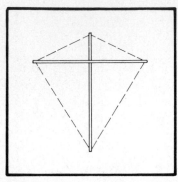

Structural form

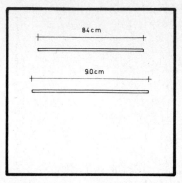

Measure spars carefully

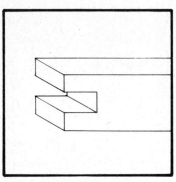

Notch ends of both spars

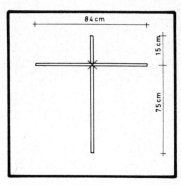

Tie short spar to spine

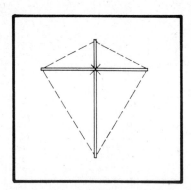

Tie line round frame

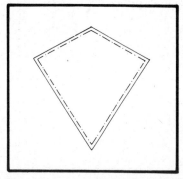

Cut out cover allowing hem all round

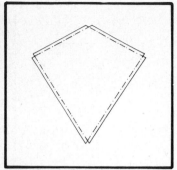

Nick corners of hem to allow turning

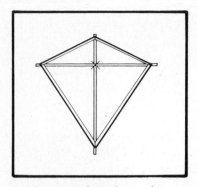

Attach cover to frame by turning and glueing down hem

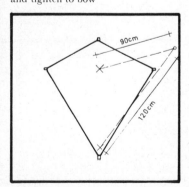

Tie line along back of cross-spar and tighten to bow

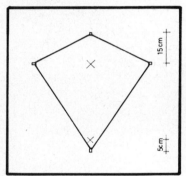

Mark 2 bridle points

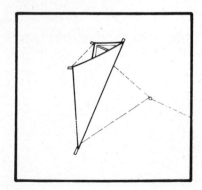

Fix 2-leg bridle

Position for launching

Sled kite

This most recently designed kite was first developed in America. It came from experiments for improving parachutes. Flies well in all winds.

Materials required
Spars – square section hardwood or softwood or bamboo
Two spars 90 cm × 0.6 cm

Cover 100 cm × 100 cm
200 gauge polythene or PVC

Adhesive tape
Metal eyelets
Line

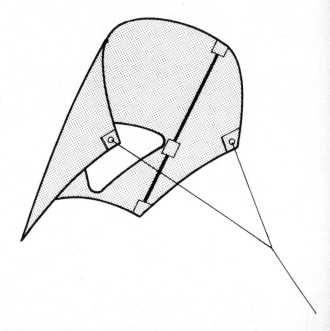

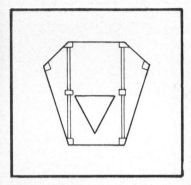

Structural form

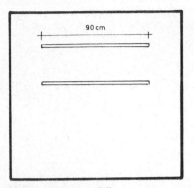

90 cm

Measure spars carefully

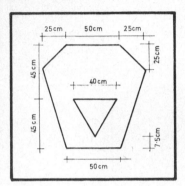

25cm 50cm 25cm

45 cm

25 cm

40 cm

45 cm

7·5cm

50 cm

Cut out cover

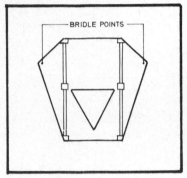

BRIDLE POINTS

Lay spars on cover and stick down
with adhesive tape

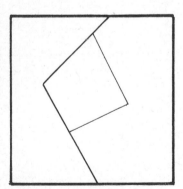

Reinforce bridle points with adhesive
tape

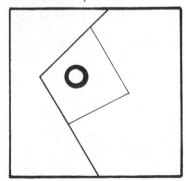

Punch bridle holes and reinforce with
metal eyelets

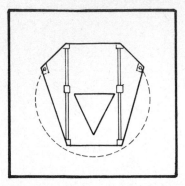

Fix 360 cm bridle as shown

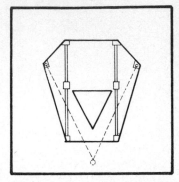

Tie knot at exact centre of bridle
allowing loop for attaching flying line

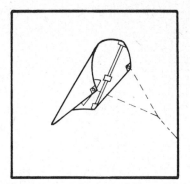

In flight

Hexagonal kite

A traditional Chinese design which often carried the image of a warrior. Flies well in moderate winds.

Materials required
Spars – square section hardwood or softwood
Three spars 75 cm × 0.6 cm

Cover 80 cm × 80 cm
Tissue paper or crepe paper

Two tails – paper streamers 300 cm × 5 cm each

Glue
Line
Towing ring

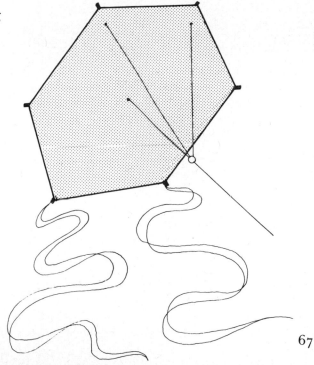

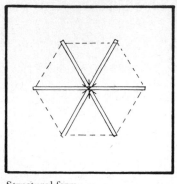

Structural form

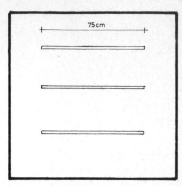

Measure spars carefully

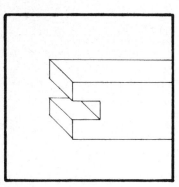

Notch ends of spars

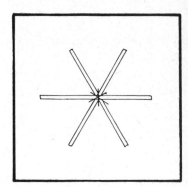

Tie spars together at centres

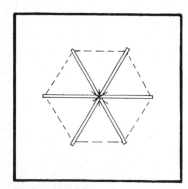

Tie line round frame, keeping ends of spars equidistant

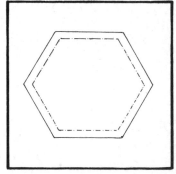

Cut out cover, allowing hem all round

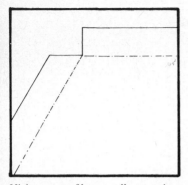

Nick corners of hem to allow turning

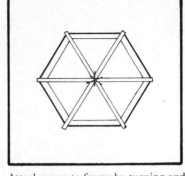

Attach cover to frame by turning and glueing down hem

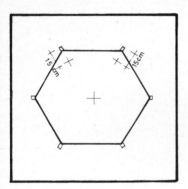

Mark 3 bridle points

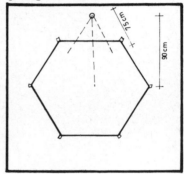

Fix 3-leg bridle

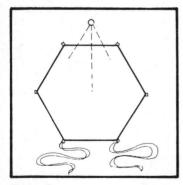

Fix 2 tails

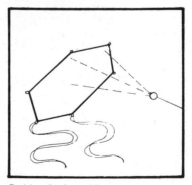

Position for launching

69

Umbrella kite

Adapted from the hexagonal kite, the bowing helps stability.
Good flier in most winds.

Materials required
Spars – square section hardwood or softwood
Four spars 90 cm × 0.6 cm

Cover 100 cm × 100 cm
Lightweight cloth or tissue paper or crepe paper

Three tails – paper streamers 300 cm × 5 cm each

Line
Glue
Towing ring

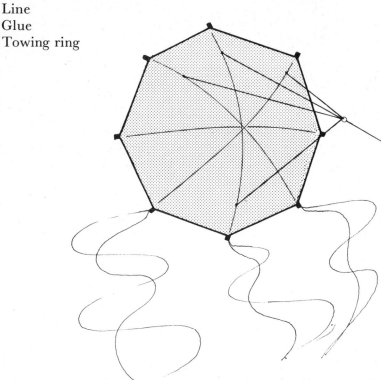

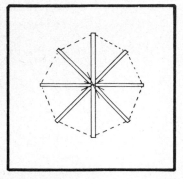

Structural form

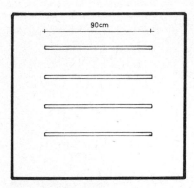

Measure spars carefully

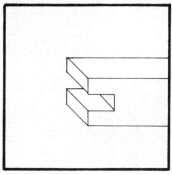

Notch ends of spars

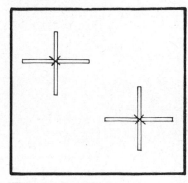

Tie pairs of spars at centres

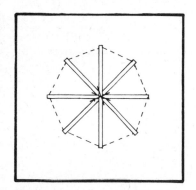

Tie spar pairs together and tie line
round frame

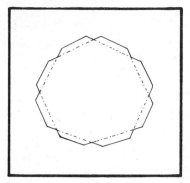

Cut out cover allowing hem all round.
Nick corners of hem to allow turning

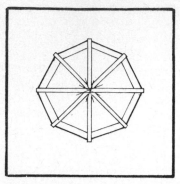

Attach cover to frame by turning
over and glueing down hem

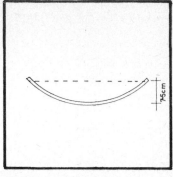

Tie line along each spar at back
and tighten bow

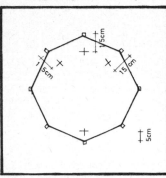

Mark 4 bridle points

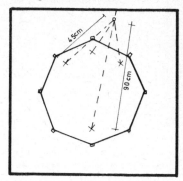

Fix 4-leg bridle. Top 3 legs of
equal length

Attach 3 tails

In flight

Eight-pointed star

A traditional Chinese design – possibly representing a star or sun. Flies well in moderate winds and lends itself to elaborate decoration.

Materials required
Spars – square section hardwood or softwood
Four spars 60 cm × 0.6 cm

Cover 65 cm × 65 cm
Tissue paper or crepe paper or lightweight cloth

Three tails – paper streamers 300 cm × 5 cm each

Line
Glue
Towing ring

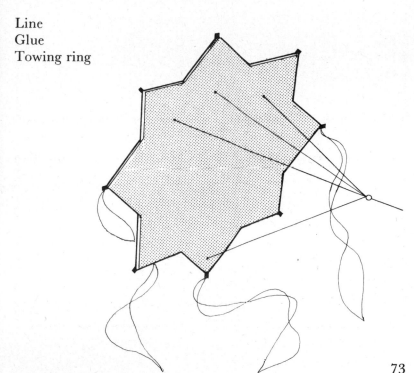

73

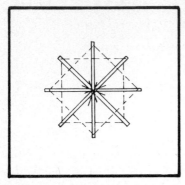

Structural form

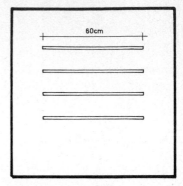

Measure spars carefully

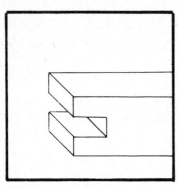

Notch ends of spars

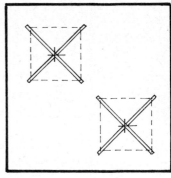

Tie spars together in pairs and
tie line round each pair

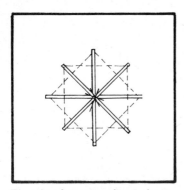

Tie pairs of spars together as shown

Fix centre joint securely with glue

Cut out cover allowing hem all round

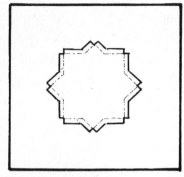

Nick corners of hem to allow turning

Attach cover to frame by turning
and glueing down hem

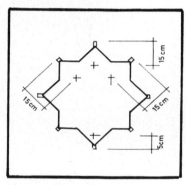

Mark 4 bridle points

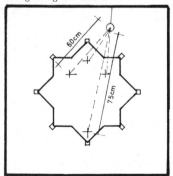

Fix 4-leg bridle. Top 3 legs of equal
length

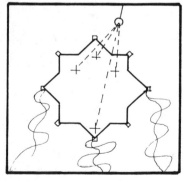

Attach 3 tails

Korean kite

A traditional fighting kite, using glass-coated line for attacking an opponent's line. The hole in the centre of the kite removes the need for a tail.

Materials required
Spars – square section hardwood or softwood or bamboo or split cane
Two spars 110 cm × 0.6 cm
One spar 90 cm × 0.6 cm
Two spars 60 cm × 0.6 cm

Cover 95 cm × 65 cm
Lightweight cloth or tissue paper or crepe paper

Line
Glue
Towing ring

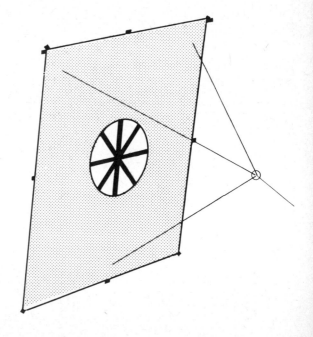

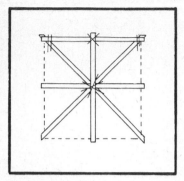

Structural form

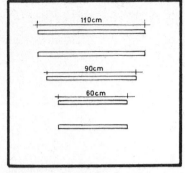

Measure spars carefully

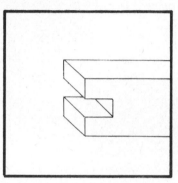

Notch ends of spars

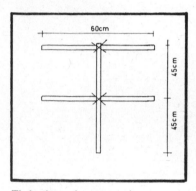

Tie horizontal spars to spine

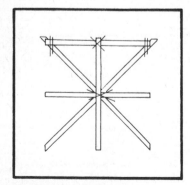

Tie diagonal cross-spars

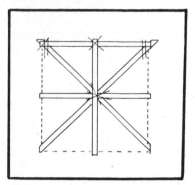

Tie line round frame

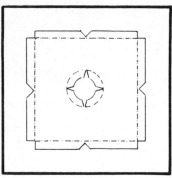

Cut out cover allowing hem all round

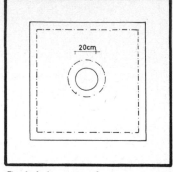

Cut hole in centre of cover

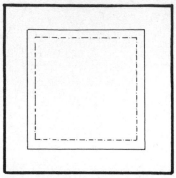

Nick corners of hem to allow turning

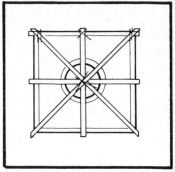

Attach cover to frame by turning and glueing down hem

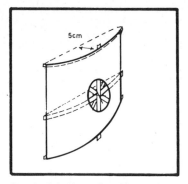

Bow both horizontal cross-spars

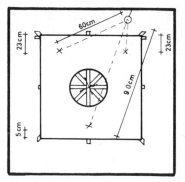

Fix 3-leg bridle. Top 2 legs of equal length

Japanese kite

Traditional design representing a tree. Like most Japanese kites it is designed for a particular seasonal festival, in this case the spring celebration. Flies well in moderate winds.

Materials required
Spars – split cane or bamboo
One spar 105 cm × 0.6 cm
Two spars 90 cm × 0.45 cm
Two spars 70 cm × 0.45 cm
Two spars 45 cm × 0.45 cm

Cover 75 cm × 95 cm
Tissue paper or lightweight cloth

Tail – paper streamer 9 m × 5 cm

Line
Glue
Towing ring

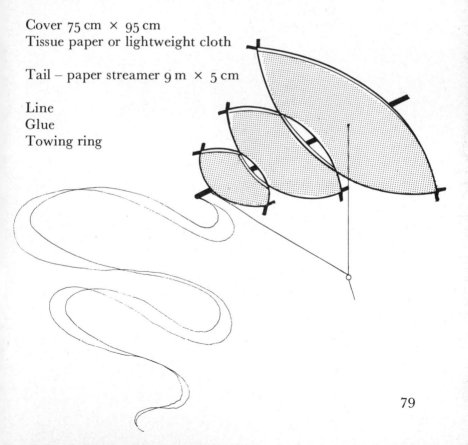

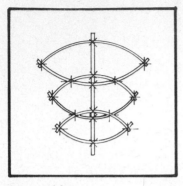

Structural form

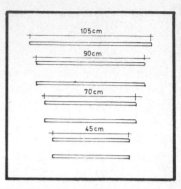

Measure spars carefully

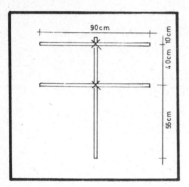

Tie spars securely on top of spine

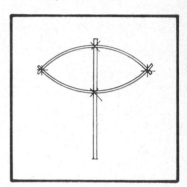

Bow together and tie securely

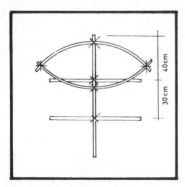

Tie second pair of spars to
underside of spine

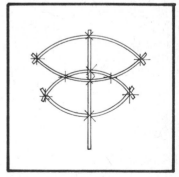

Bow spars together and tie
securely

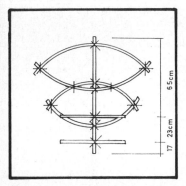

Tie third pair of spars on top of spine

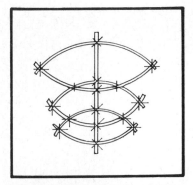

Bow spars together and tie securely

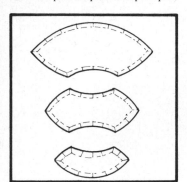

Cut out 3 covers allowing hem all
round and nick hems to allow turning

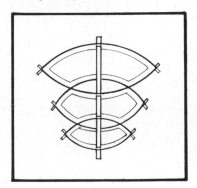

Attach covers to frame

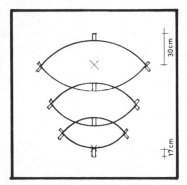

Mark 2 bridle points

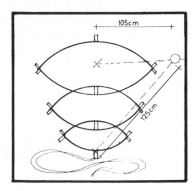

Fix 2-leg bridle and tail

Nagasaki fighting kite

Traditional Japanese fighting kite with excellent manoeuvrability and speed. The line was coated with ground glass to cut an opponent's line. Flies well in most winds. A tail can be added for increased stability.

Materials required
Spars – split cane or bamboo
One spar 90 cm × 0.6 cm
One spar 110 cm × 0.6 cm

Cover 100 cm × 100 cm
Lightweight cloth or tissue paper or crepe paper

Line
Glue
Towing ring

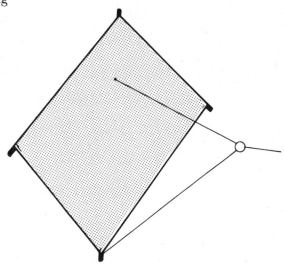

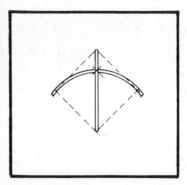

Structural form

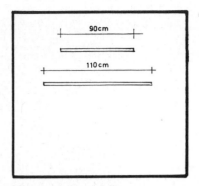

Measure spars carefully

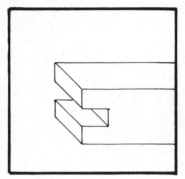

Notch ends of spars

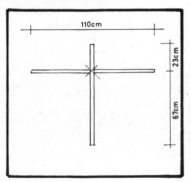

Tie cross-spar to spine

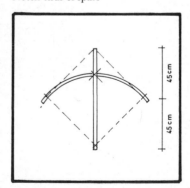

Tie line round frame bowing
cross-spar till ends are level with
centre of spine

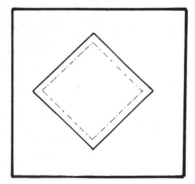

Cut out cover allowing hem
all round

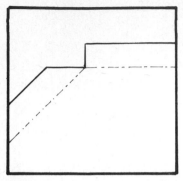

Nick corners of hem to allow turning

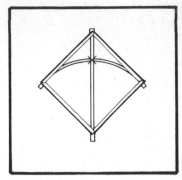

Attach cover to frame by turning and glueing down hem

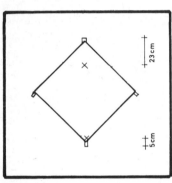

Mark 2 bridle points

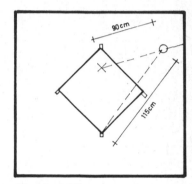

Fix 2-leg bridle

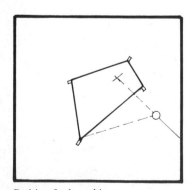

Position for launching

Kites in flight

Aeroplane kite

The Western innovation of the fin gives this kite increased stability, acting like the keel of a boat. Flies well at a great height in moderate winds.

Materials required
Spars – square section hardwood or softwood or bamboo
One spar 120 cm × 0.6 cm
One spar 90 cm × 0.6 cm
One spar 60 cm × 0.6 cm
One spar 20 cm × 0.6 cm

Cover 95 cm × 125 cm
Lightweight cloth or tissue paper or crepe paper

Cloth adhesive tape
Line
Glue
Towing ring

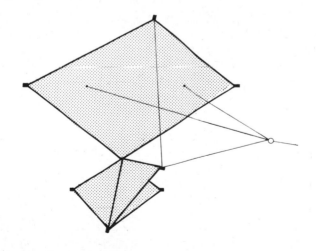

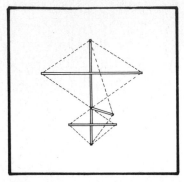

Structural form

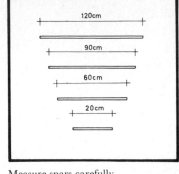

Measure spars carefully

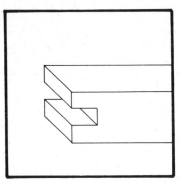

Notch ends of spars, but one end only of shortest

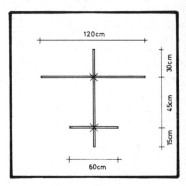

Tie wing spars to spine

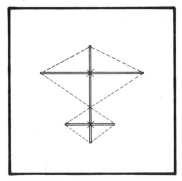

Tie line round frame as shown

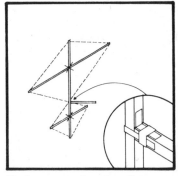

Fix fin spar to spine where lines cross, using cloth adhesive tape

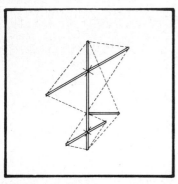

Tie line to hold fin spar steady

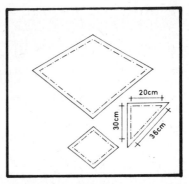

Cut out covers allowing hem all round

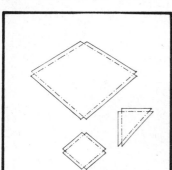

Nick corners of hem to allow turning

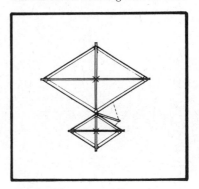

Attach main covers to frame by
turning and glueing down hem

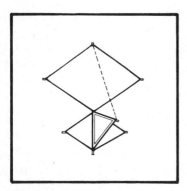

Attach fin cover

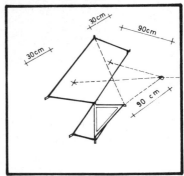

Fix 3-leg bridle. Top two legs of
equal length

Pyramid kite

Developed by Alexander Graham Bell at the turn of the century as part of his experiments into manflight. Flies well in high winds.

Materials required
Spars – square section hardwood or softwood
Six spars 75 cm × 0.6 cm

Cover 160 cm × 80 cm
Lightweight cloth or tissue paper or crepe paper

Line
Glue
Towing ring

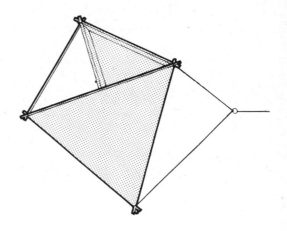

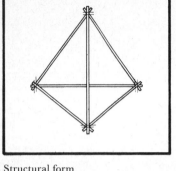

Structural form

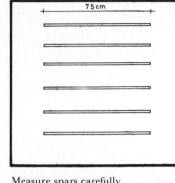

Measure spars carefully

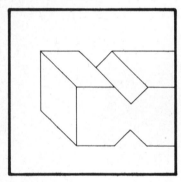

Notch ends of spars

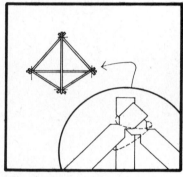

Tie spars firmly together making
pyramid shape

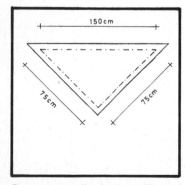

Cut out cover allowing hem all round

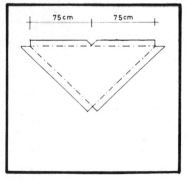

Nick corners of hem to allow turning

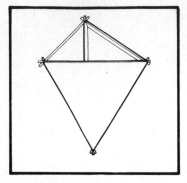

Attach cover to frame by turning
and glueing down hem

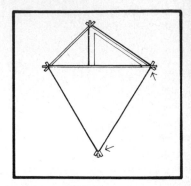

Mark 2 bridle points

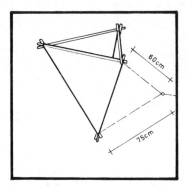

60 cm

75 cm

Fix 2-leg bridle

Box kite

Invented by Hargrave in Australia in the late nineteenth century and was used as part of the RAF Sea Rescue equipment for carrying wireless aerials. Very stable in moderate and heavy winds.

Materials required
Spars – square section hardwood or softwood
Four spars 90 cm × 0.6 cm
Four spars 43 cm × 0.6 cm

Cover 137 cm × 70 cm
Lightweight cloth

Needle and cotton
Line
Glue

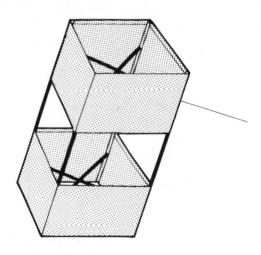

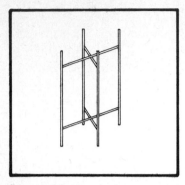

Structural form

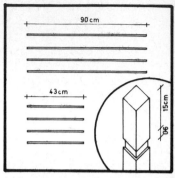

Measure spars carefully and notch both ends of long spars as shown

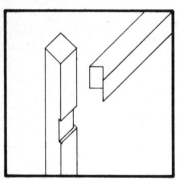

Notch ends of cross-spars to fit notches in long spars

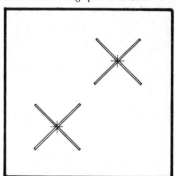

Tie pairs of cross-spars at centres

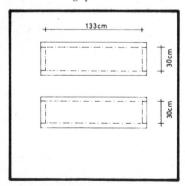

Cut covers allowing hems. Turn and sew down top and bottom hems of each cover

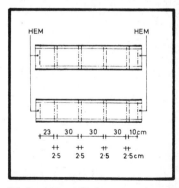

Mark position of long spar pockets

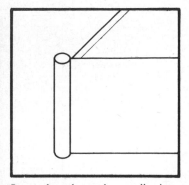

Sew each pocket as shown, allowing room to hold long spar

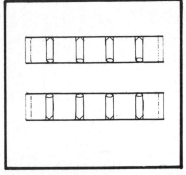

Stitch closed one end of each pocket as shown

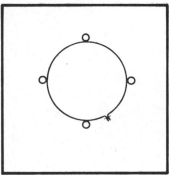

Sew together ends of each cover keeping pockets equidistant

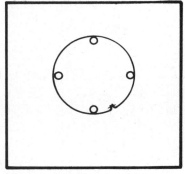

Turn covers inside out and insert long spars

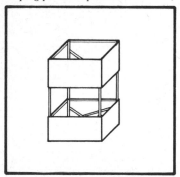

Slit pockets over cross-spar notches. Push cross-spars into place

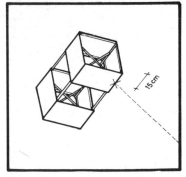

Attach flying line to tying point

93

Bird kite

Adapted from traditional Chinese/Malaysian design. It hovers at a great height looking like a bird of prey and is sometimes used by Eastern farmers as a bird scare. Flies well in moderate winds.

Materials required
Spars – square section hardwood or softwood or split cane or bamboo
One spar 110 cm × 0.6 cm
Two spars 90 cm × 0.6 cm
One spar 17 cm × 0.6 cm

Cover 90 cm × 90 cm
Lightweight cloth or crepe paper or tissue paper

Two tails – paper streamers 12 m × 5 cm each

Line
Glue
Towing ring

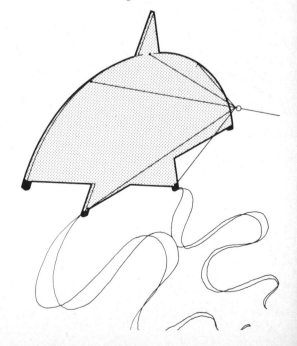

Structural form

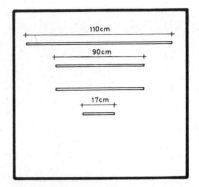

Measure spars carefully

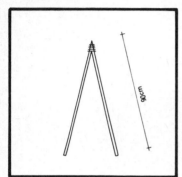

Tie spars together at one end.
See detail

Detail. Spar ends must be shaved
down to ensure neat mitre joint,
then glue and tie

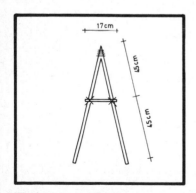

Tie short spar as shown

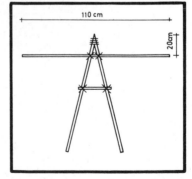

Tie wing spar across frame as shown

95

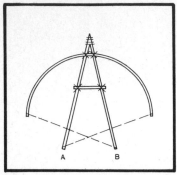

Bow wing spar by tying back to points A and B

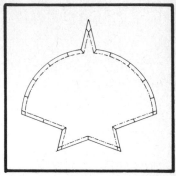

Cut out cover allowing hem all round and nick hem to allow turning

Attach cover to frame by turning and glueing down hem

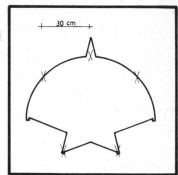

Mark 5 bridle points

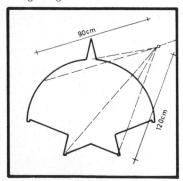

Fix 5-leg bridle. Top 3 legs and bottom 2 legs of equal length

Attach two tails

Marconi kite

Developed by Marconi, the inventor of the wireless, and used in his famous first intercontinental radio link-up to carry the aerial. A difficult kite to make well but is capable of fine adjustment and is a very efficient flying machine. Flies in moderate to heavy winds.

Materials required
Spars – square section hardwood or softwood
Two spars 120 cm × 0.6 cm
One spar 20 cm × 0.6 cm

Cover 120 cm × 120 cm
Lightweight cloth
Twelve tabs 15 cm × 0.6 cm each (cotton tape)
Cloth-reinforced adhesive tape

Needle and cotton
Line
Glue
Towing ring

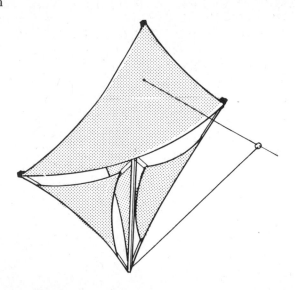

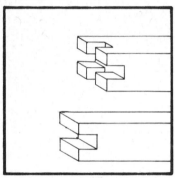

Structural form

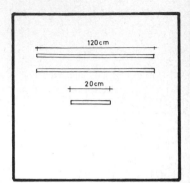

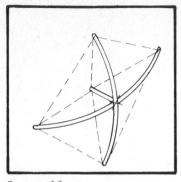

Notch ends of long spars and cross-
notch one end only of short spar

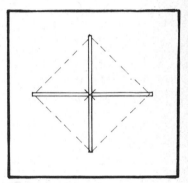

Tie long spars together at centres
and tie line round frame

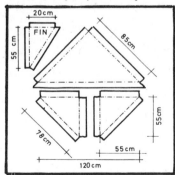

Cut out covers allowing hems all
round and nick all corners to
allow turning

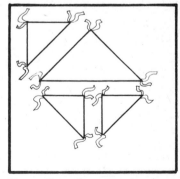

Turn under and sew down hems.
Stitch on tabs for fixing covers
to frame

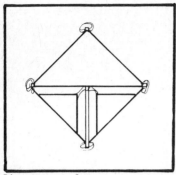

Lie covers over frame to ensure correct fit. Do not attach yet

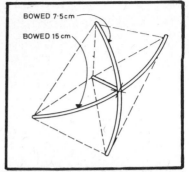

Fix fin spar to back of kite as in next diagram and bow spars as shown

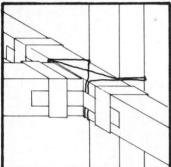

Fix fin spar to spine using cloth-reinforced adhesive tape

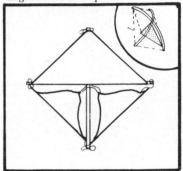

Tie on covers, including fin cover at back

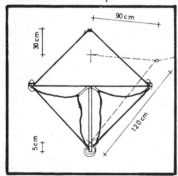

Fix 2-leg bridle

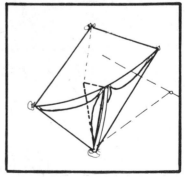

Bottom flaps should be loose in light winds and tight in heavy winds. Main cover and fin cover always tight

Triangulated box kite

Adapted from Hargrave's Box Kite. It is stable in heavy winds.

Materials required
Spars – square section hardwood or softwood
Three spars 90 cm × 0.6 cm
Six spars 38 cm × 0.6 cm

Cover 115 cm × 65 cm
Lightweight cloth
Twelve tabs 15 cm × 0.6 cm each (cotton tape)

Needle and cotton
Line
Glue

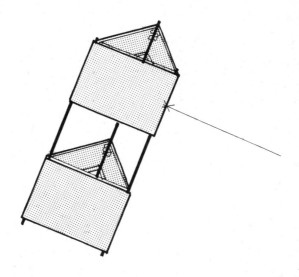

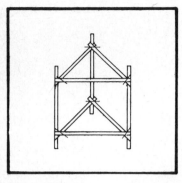

Structural form

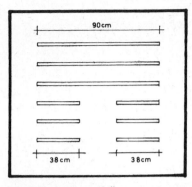

Measure spars carefully

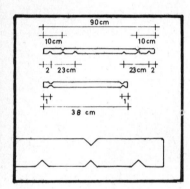

Notch ends of all spars as shown

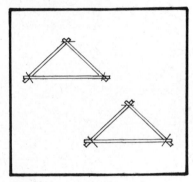

Tie short spars together to form
2 triangles

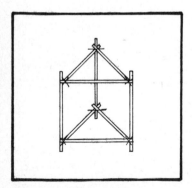

Tie triangles to vertical spars.
Glue joints

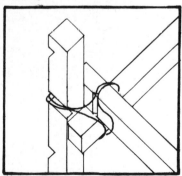

Detail. Triangles tied to vertical spars

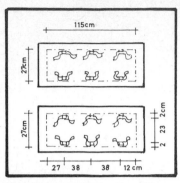

Cut out covers allowing hem all round. Stitch down hems, sew on tabs as shown

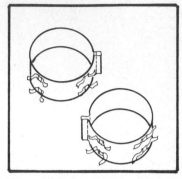

Sew ends of covers together to fit kite frame firmly with tabs outside

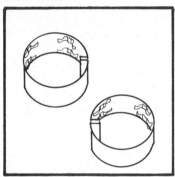

Turn covers outside in

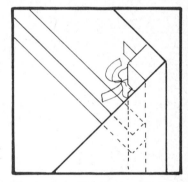

Tie on covers with tabs round notches

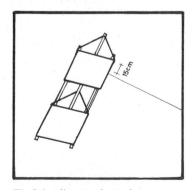

Fix flying line to tying point

In flight

Conyne kite

The Conyne kite, named after its inventor Silas J. Conyne, is sometimes called the French Military kite, because it was first used by the French army during the 1914–18 war. The kite is made up of plane and angled surfaces. It is a good medium- to heavy-weather kite and will fly in winds of 10 to 25 knots.

Materials required
Spars – square section hardwood or softwood
Four spars 100 cm × 0.6 cm
One spar 30 cm × 0.6 cm

Cover 120 cm × 120 cm
Lightweight cloth

Pockets 30 cm × 30 cm lightweight canvas or reinforced nylon

Needle and cotton
Line
Towing ring

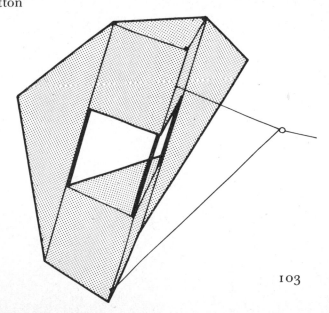

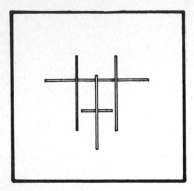

Structural form

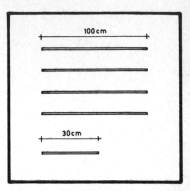

Measure spars carefully

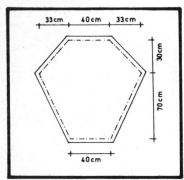

Cut out main covering allowing
hem all round

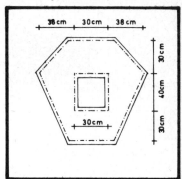

Cut out central hole allowing
hem all round

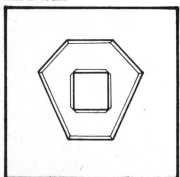

Nick all corners of hems. Then
turn over and sew down hems

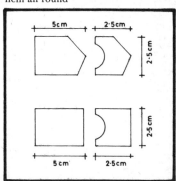

Cut out canvas pocket shapes –
4 of each

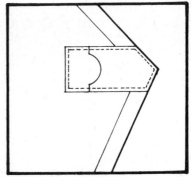

Mark position of spar pockets on back
of cover and sew down firmly. See detail

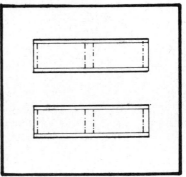

Detail of spar pockets

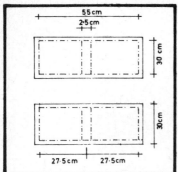

Cut out small covers and mark
positions for central spar pocket

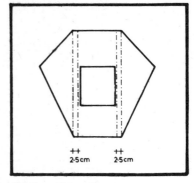

Turn over and sew down top and
bottom hems of each small cover

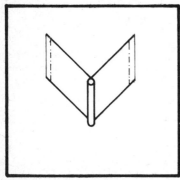

Sew central spar pocket to hold
spar firmly

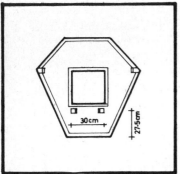

Mark positions of long spar
pockets on front of main cover

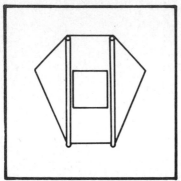

Sew spar pockets to hold spars
firmly

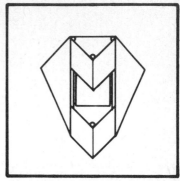

Sew small covers to main cover.
See detail

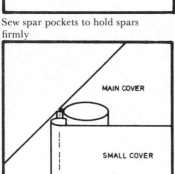

Detail of how to sew small cover
to main cover

MAIN COVER

SMALL COVER

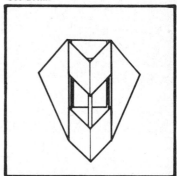

Insert all long spars and sew
pocket ends closed

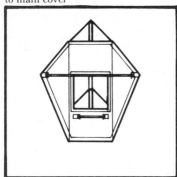

Insert horizontal spars across
back of main cover

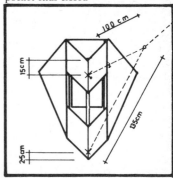

Mark bridle points and fix
2-leg bridle

Multicell tetrahedral kite

This is an extended version of the single-cell kite and can be extended still further. Alexander Graham Bell built a kite with many hundreds of cells. Needs a high wind for good flight.

Materials required
Spars – square section hardwood or softwood
Seven spars 140 cm × 0.6 cm
Twelve spars 67 cm × 0.6 cm

Cover 530 cm × 85 cm
Lightweight cloth

Corner brackets 0.3 cm plywood
Approx. 30 cm × 30 cm

Panel pins
Cloth-reinforced adhesive 5 cm tape
Line
Glue
Towing ring

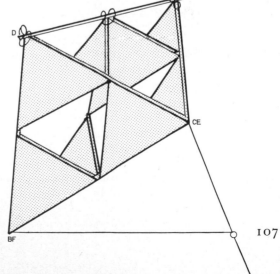

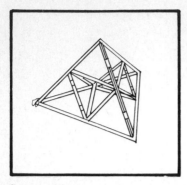

Structural form

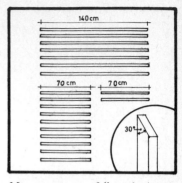

Measure spars carefully and mitre all ends to an angle of 30°

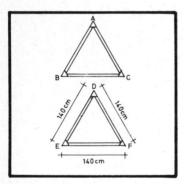

Join long spars to form 2 triangles. See detail

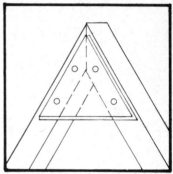

Detail. Cut corner brackets and glue and pin to spars

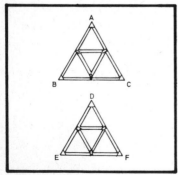

Attach internal spars as shown. See detail

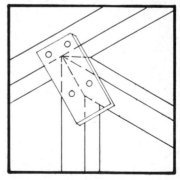

Detail. Cut corner brackets and glue and pin to spars

Make up remaining spars into
2 triangles. See detail

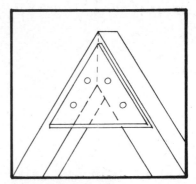

Detail. Cut corner brackets and
glue and pin to spars.

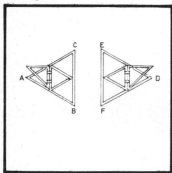

Using adhesive tape attach triangles
to main frames as shown. See detail

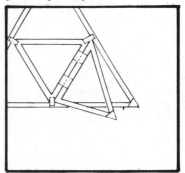

Detail of adhesive tape hinge

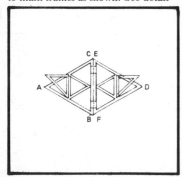

Hinge main frames together as shown.
See detail

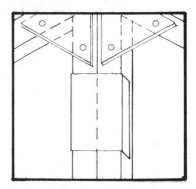

Detail of adhesive tape hinge

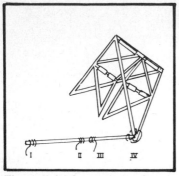

Tie remaining long spar to main
frame as shown. See details

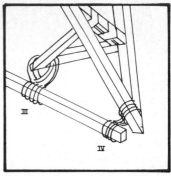

Detail of tying long spar to main
frame

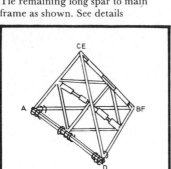

Detail of structure without cover
showing long spar tied to frame

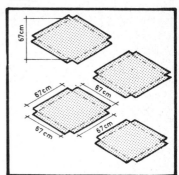

Cut out 4 equal covers allowing
hems all round

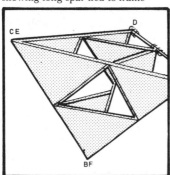

Tack or glue covers turning hems
round spars

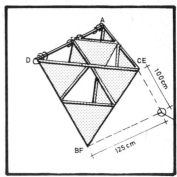

Attach 2-leg bridle to bridle points

More Beaver Books

We hope you have enjoyed this Beaver Book. Here are some of the other titles:

The Beaver Book of Games A Beaver original. George and Cornelia Kay describe dozens of games to play indoors and outdoors, including all the old favourites plus lots of new ones. Illustrated by Robin Anderson

The Pool of Fire The last book of John Christopher's 'Tripods' trilogy which brings to a dramatic climax the story of the struggle to overthrow the Masters, invaders from outer space. The first two books are *The White Mountains* and *The City of Gold and Lead*, both published in Beavers

Amazing But True A collection of stories about amazing people, places and events, from the Man in the Iron Mask to the stone statues on Easter Island and the unsolved mystery of the *Mary Celeste*; illustrated throughout

The Beaver Book of Brain Ticklers A Beaver original. Intriguing puzzles and teasers of a mathematical type invented by Charles Booth-Jones; illustrated with cartoons, diagrams and line drawings

The Sword of the Wilderness Elizabeth Coatsworth's exciting story about a young boy captured by Indians, set at the time of the early settlement of North America

New Beavers are published every month and if you would like the *Beaver Bulletin* – which gives all the details – please send a large stamped addressed envelope to:

Beaver Bulletin
The Hamlyn Group
Astronaut House
Feltham
Middlesex TW14 9AR

353362